MUNDANE MUSINGS

REFLECTIONS ON DREAMS AND DETOURS

ANN MARIA GEORGE

BookLeaf
Publishing

India | USA | UK

Made with ❤ on the BookLeaf Publishing Platform
www.bookleafpub.in
www.bookleafpub.com

Dedication

To THOMAS,HANNAH & EMMA,
To my parents,siblings,friends and every soul who
crossed paths...
Thank you for adding colours,chaos and clarity to my
life...
This book is,in parts,yours too...

Preface

Thirties arrives quietly, then all at once. It is both a reckoning and a renewal—a place where the past lingers, the present demands, and the future whispers its uncertainties. These poems are the musings of a heart that has lived, loved, questioned, and grown. They are glimpses into moments of clarity and doubt, of nostalgia and acceptance, of standing still and moving forward.
This collection is not about resolutions or regrets, but about reflection. About the way time reshapes us, softens some edges, and sharpens others. It is about the weight of experience and the lightness of letting go.
If you find yourself within these pages, know that you are not alone. These words are for those who have paused to wonder where they've been, who they've become, and where they're going. For those who understand that some pauses are not endings, but an unfolding.
May these musings bring you comfort, clarity, or simply the reassurance that the journey is still yours to write.
Welcome to *Mundane Musings...*

Acknowledgements

This book exists because of you—Thomas—my anchor, my love, and the quiet force behind every word I write. Your belief in me, even when I doubted myself, has been the foundation of this journey. Without you, *Mundane Musings* would have remained just some—musings, never finding their way to these pages. Thank you for being my greatest reason and my greatest support.

To my children, who keep me on my toes and remind me that life is beautifully unpredictable. You challenge me, inspire me, and fill my world with meaning.

To Teena and Josu, who never let me get too lost in my own thoughts—thank you for the reality checks, the laughter, and the reminders of where I come from.

To my daily cups of coffee—because let's be honest, none of this would be possible without you. You fuel both my body and my thoughts, one sip at a time.

And to the reader—you, who have picked up this book and stepped into these musings with me—thank you. Your time, your presence in these pages, means more than words can say.

Love,

Ann

1. RAIN

The drops stirred the depths of my soul,
Cleansing the weariness of endless days,
As scattered thoughts bubbled and swirled,
Ready to spill in a cascade of words.
A cool breeze kissed my face,
Carrying with it a distant smile,
Awakening a desire, a love newly found.
The world resonates with my inner song.
The wounded faces, the scarred hearts,
The weary smiles, the mocking laughter,
The burdens, the tension, the heavy regrets,
All absorbed in the endless rain of infinity.
A quiet longing, a nameless joy,
Twisting and soaring, higher and higher still,
Until my soul finds its haven deep within,
Far from the clamor, far from the world,
Awaiting to rejoice with the new found self

2. FLAWED LOVE

Dwelling in the quiet echoes of your calming voice,
I smile,My dearest friend, my heart's first choice.
Through a mirror dimmed and scarred,
Our love reflects, though marred,
Blemished glass, blurred to the eye,
Yet through it, we see—just you and I.
We love, we cherish, we gave life breath,
In silence, promises weave their thread.
Unseen joys and surprises untold,
In the midst of what we can't behold.
Uncertainty lingers, yet we remain,
A constant truth amidst the strain.
For in every flaw, our love is cast,
A timeless bond, forever vast.
Opposites we are, yet perfectly entwined,
In your soft-spoken decibel, true love I find.
You've witnessed my lows, seen me unseen
Together we've built a bond so serene.
With no grand displays, just simple,
sweet little things makes our love complete.

Plans may falter, but love will prevail,
Leading us on a dreamy, destined trail.
Let's embrace the moments, big and small,
For with you, my love, I cherish it all.

3. FAITH

When shadows loom and whispers foretell,
When my heart feels heavy, for no clear reason
I pray, for I am woven that way—
And oh, the solace it brings to my day.
Through storms that rise and tides that swell,
I find my anchor; I find myself.
Whatever may come, I stand steadfast,
For in my faith, I swim and survive.

When tasks unfold, and plans take shape,
When all is done, no loose ends escape,
Still, I pray, for I am woven that way,
Incomplete without that sacred name.
A single chant, a whispered plea,
Completes the circle inside of me.
This ritual breathes life anew,
For that is my faith, strong and true.

When joy abounds and blessings fall,
When praises rise and I feel tall,

Sisterhood is not the clamor of shared gossip,
but the solace of shared burdens.
It's the ones who praise your smallest win,
and love you without judgements.

To the friends from my past and present
to the random souls who stay without reason,
to those who need no daily check-ins,
but whose hearts I know just like that

Thank you for being my haven, my kin.
Your warmth, greater than words can tell.
Your mere existence made my mundane life
Joyful,meaningful and beautiful.

5. DIVISION

The chasm between rich and poor will linger long,
For judgments are cast not on deeds but gold once
owned.
From humble roots, you climb with tireless might,
Yet whispers linger, though you shine so bright.
In the halls of wealth, your worth is often gauged
By lineage,money and by the past you engaged.
The rich, though flawed, remain unseen, unscathed
But echoes of your gone poverty are eternally engraved .
Rightly so,prophets' value in their lands is slight,
While the world sing your praises with delight.
Validation from strangers may soothe the sting,
For respect, not wealth, is the treasure you seek to bring.

6. HOME

We dreamt of walls that would cradle our soul,
Brick by brick, we built it whole.
A door to promise, a roof of pride,
Yet life's demands took me far from its side.

A home I called mine, yet fleeting my stay,
Work carried me miles, day after day.
Then came marriage, a new chapter begun,
And slowly, my first home felt distant.

I returned as a guest, though it was my own,
They catered with love, but felt a little odd
Secrets were kept, burdens disguised,
I learned of them later, with settled sighs.

With my firstborn, I lived there once more,
Months of joy, a brief restore.
But as time moved on, its halls became
A shadowy echo of a cherished name.

Then with my second, I lingered awhile,
Felt its warmth, but sensed the exile.
For it's mine, yet not mine, a bittersweet air,
A place I belong, yet not fully there.

Now I build anew, with partner and kids,
A house where fresh memories begin.
But my first home stays, like a star in the night,
A constant, a comfort, a lighthouse.

Though it fades to the background,
It's the root of my story, where my heart is.
And while my new home becomes my all,
My first will always answer my call.

7. MOTHERHOOD IN PLURAL

With one, the rules are written clear,
Whole of us revolves around one tiny being.
A lulluby for every cry,sung through the night,
Every hunger met, every fear made right.

But then comes two, and the world divides,
A single heart stretched on both sides.
Not a matter of first or second born,
But the dance of love, both weary and worn.

One hand feeds while the other soothes,
One voice sings while the other moves.
Two cries echo, each a plea,
"Hold me now, hold only me now."

The newborn stirs with needs untold,
The toddler's tantrums loud and bold.
Each moment split, each choice a fight,
To balance love, both day and night.

No rulebook guides this intricate art,
To nurture two from a single heart.
With every tear and every smile,
We exhaust like we ran a mile.

Motherhood in plurals is a constant race,
A tug-of-war for a single embrace.
But though we falter, though we bend,
Love's infinite, First or second.

8. DECEMBER DREAMS

I have always loved December's glow,
A month of wonders, a magical season..
I marveled at stars in their shimmering hue.
Now gram updates tell us all loved it too.

Warm lights adorned the velvet night,
Giving shadows a pulse, a breath, a life..
I loved the cold, the midnight mass,
The secret gifts and the real christmas cards .

Childhood's magic, wrapped in a bow,
Fades with time, but lingers still deep below
For, as adults, we still revive
That Christmas spark,to keep dreams alive.

We hang stockings, we trim the tree,
We craft the cribs and hang the stars
We light the homes, we replay the tales,
Chasing a hope that never pales.

Is it the miracle we yearn to see,
Or the dreams of a child we long to be?
Dreams that shifted as years passed by,
Detoured by life, yet still reside.

Perhaps in living the dream once dreamed,
The magic feels even more redeemed.
For though I say it's for my child's delight,
These are my memories, my starlit night.

So I craft the magic, year by year,
For the child in me who still holds it dear.
December whispers, with stars that gleam,
A season of love, and a heart's old dream.

9. DEATH

Some deaths strike with aching force,
Not from closeness, but from shared course.
You see the lives the mourners bear,
And feel the weight of their despair,
Imagining the pain, the grief and the tears,
If such news came while cradling your baby,
Would you freeze, or would you compose?
Could you stifle the cries that rise,
For your child's sake, hide the demise?
It's not how you endure the end,
But how the small triggers extend.
Time, I believe, does not heal,
It buries the wounds,ready to surface,
With a reminder that hurts so much.
The intensity may wane,but the mark remains
Like a scar, a part of your tale,
A silent reminder of sorrow's trail..

10. MONUMENT

A building stands ,where stories breathe
Shops that cradle generations beneath.
Brick by brick, before cement and paint,
Ancestral hands shaped this enduring space.

Three generations, their dreams encased,
In walls that time itself has traced .
Witness to the barter of goods and cheer,
Shelter for wanderers, landmark for the lost.

A tailor once stitched dreams with thread,
A tea shop where steaming tales were spread.
Evenings hummed with a local club's cheer,
Debates and laughter lingered here.

It watched the roads grow, winding wide,
Saw the march of time on every side.
New buildings rise, old faces fade,
Yet here it stands, where roots were laid.

The sun scorched high, the rain poured too,
Its shade and refuge, a place to go.
Feet of many have tread its ground,
Echoes of voices still resound.

Silent sentinel, steadfast and true,
A monument to all it knew.
Brick by brick, it holds the past,
A timeless structure, built to last.

11. SEA OF LIGHTS

The church stands bright in a sea of lights,
Colors dancing against the night.
Footsteps echo on the old stone way,
The band matching the heartbeats rhythm.

A child's delight in a sweet ice cream,
Fireworks bursting like a fleeting dream.
The tiny shops with treasures untold,
Bangles and toys for a few coins those days.

The crowd, the cheer, the rustling song,
The best of dresses, the walk so long.
Processions grand, the banners high,
Candles glowing against the sky.

Faces new and old we meet,
Smiles exchanged on bustling streets.
In every corner, joy unfurls,
A festival wrapped in lights and smiles.

Now I stand with hands so small,
Little fingers in mine held close.
I guide them through this world so bright,
A piece of my past in their present light.

One day, when time has flown away,
May they return on some quiet day.
And find, within their heart's embrace,
A love found in togetherness of family.

12. THE ART OF UNLEARNING

They taught me to walk the path often took,
Lined with rules, shaped by judgment's wrath.
Be perfect, they said, be polished, be wise,
Hide the mess, wear the disguise.

They called us the quiet, the gentle, the good,
Obedient ,they labelled us from childhood
We followed their voices "come here, go there"
Never a question, never a stare, just fear.

Teenage years, a storm held tight,
Crushes burn and hearts take flight.
Anger simmers, wild and deep,
Yet we never spoke and let go the "good tag".

In social circles, I played the charade,
A well-organized girl in a masquerade.
Yet the world showed me, through voices kind,
That being myself was the freedom I missed.

Life whispered truths the world ignored,
That instinct, not order, is what we're born for.
Life runs not by schedules or rules, nor a flawless plan,
But by moments unseen, where I simply began.

Not all paths are straight, not all answers clear,
What works for one may not for another.
The vastness of life unfolded its wings,
Thank God for those who changed my notions.

I will not shape my kids with my past,
Nor bind them tight, nor hold them fast.
No weight of labels, harsh and strong,
No whispered rule of right and wrong.

I'll let them wander, let them see,
Let them question, let them be.
With kindness taught and hearts set free,
They'll grow into the best of them, not me.

So here I stand, with roots shaken,
Planting new seeds in unfamiliar ground.
Unlearning the fear, the judgment, the strife,
And trusting my heart to guide my life.

13. MY FAVOURITE THINGS

Now, when I think back, I wonder if my favorite things
were ever mine.
Were they the things I had, Or the things they said was
best for me?
I only remember the things they said no to, And those-
those became my favorites.

The Barbie doll in the glass shelf,
The one with the tiny pink car,
I never held her, never played,
But she was my favorite toy—
The one I never had.

The bakery window, lined with sweets,
Glazed and golden, soft and bright,
But my plate held only mundane delicacies
Yet, in my heart, the sweet things were my favorite
things.

The elegant dresses on mannequins,
Flowing, sparkling, meant for someone else.
I wore what was needed, what was enough, But my
favorite clothes were always the ones beyond my reach.

My favorite color? The cheapest hue.
My favorite toy? The one that was gifted.
My favorite meal? The one that was there.
Not the rare, not the special,
But the one we could afford.

Now, I sit and think— Did I ever choose?
Did I ever know? Or were my favorite things- simply the
dreams I was never allowed to hold?

14. OCEAN'S SONG

They ask, Are you mountain or sea?
A question that everyone seems to know certainly.
For some, the peaks, the hills, thin air,
The rocks and the cliffs, get them high.

But me—I'm the waves, the night tide,
Where horizons stretch, where dreams collide.
The salt-kissed wind, the golden glow,
The place where restless spirits flow.

It's not that I hate the mountain climb,
Once, I might have called it mine.
But in these years, as time has spun,
My steps have slowed, my race is run.

Once, effort was a price I'd pay,
For a fleeting view at the top one day.
But now, I ask—why must I chase,
When beauty meets me right where I want?

The shore, it offers all I seek,
Sunrise soft, the sunset meek.
Waves that whisper, breeze so light,
A place to rest, no need for height.

No sweat, no strain, no dizzy climb,
Just space to breathe, a life in rhyme.
The mountains call the strong, the bold,
Their will like stone, their focus, mighty heights.

But me—I choose the ocean's song,
The place where ease and peace belong.
Maybe mountain lads are better, wise and free,
But this is where I'm meant to be.

15. FUTURE

I dream of a future, calm and breezy,
A cottage near the sea, painted yellow and white.
Where waves hum songs of endless peace,
And time slows down, like we do then.
Mornings begin with the scent of the tide,
Fresh air filling lungs, hearts open wide.
A stretch, a breath, a workout in sync,
Hands wrapped around warm cups,
as we sit and talk.
No rush, no race, just steady days,
Neighbors' hellos, the sun's golden rays.
A stroll through streets, a book in hand,
Stories unfolding, simple yet grand.
No screens to pull our minds away,
Just paper and ink, and words that stay.
Journals filled with thoughts so free,
Pages of life, just you and me.
Children visit, laughter flows,
Their voices echo in halls they know.
A home to call, a memory bright.

And when the years weigh on our skin,
When life starts giving final reminders,
With whatever sorrows and whatever aches,
We'll face it all, we will not break.
For by then, no walls define our place,
No longing left for homes once chased.
We are each other's shelter, our own,
A love so deep, it stands alone.
And if one day, I walk alone,
Or you sit quiet, on your own,
Even then, this love remains,
Our home, unshaken, through joy and pain.

16. SLEEP, THE LUXURY

Sleep was once so easy to find,
Long and deep, anytime,anywhere.
Afternoon naps, lazy nights,
Now just memories and lights at night.
One child wakes, the other sleeps,
A cycle of tiny hands and needs.
Feeding, bathing, playing too,
No rest for me, there's much to do.
And when at last they close their eyes,
I sip my coffee, tired but wise.
For though I crave the sleep I lack,
I cannot survive without my me time.
One day, when sleep will fill my days,
Will I miss these sleepless days??.

17. THE OMNIVERT'S DILEMMA

There are extroverts— loud, bright,
the spark in the room.
"The life of the party," they say,
watching them light up the air.
There are introverts— quiet, reserved,
a world within.
"Oh, let them be," they whisper,
knowing silence is their space.
There are ambiverts-who balances both beautifully.
A soul that shifts with place and people,
At ease with both,yet bound by none.
Then there are omniverts-whom often
people misjudge as an ambivert .
One day, the laughter spills from them,
the next, they sit in stillness.
And the world watches, confused.
"Why are you so quiet today?"
"Yesterday, you were different."
As if being both is a contradiction,

As if the self must stay still.
But don't you see? It's the circles,
the ambience, the people—
Shaping the voice, shifting the mood,
a dance between light and shade.
So don't judge— not by moments,
not by silence.
There are layers yet unseen,
chapters yet unread.
Some of us live in between.

18. EMBRACE

In my twenties, I ran, chased dreams,
Worked late,woke early,built walls with the pay
thought success meant more.
In my thirties, I slowed, heard my own breath,
Watched dust settle on trophies.
Money still mattered,but not for luxury
for safety, for learning,for the unwelcomed uncertanities.
I listen to my body now,
Feed it what keeps me whole,
move to feel alive, not just to keep up.
I learned again—like a child,
not for degrees, but for wonder.
Not for status, but for self.
I teach my children with love,
the way I wished to be taught.
Success is peace, not pressure or promotions
home is laughter, not walls nor props.
And I became calmer, not because life became easy,
but because I finally knew,what was worth the fight.
I look forward to my forties, my fifties— unburdened,

unchained,
where life is lighter, and every moment shines.

19. THE COLOURS WE PAINT

They called him a color, not a name,
A shade too dark for their cruel game.
Not a boy, not a soul, just skin,
Stamped by a world that won't let him in.

They learned it first at home, at tea,
In whispered tones of "fair" and "brown."
Rich and poor, light and dark,
Lines drawn deep, leaving marks.

And when he left, did they not see?
That kindness is not taught in degrees.
I won't teach my child the calculus and chemistry,
But kindness and empathy which no curriculum offers.

One day, may color just be a hue,
And worth be weighed in what we do.

20. BALANCE

Not asking to rise above, just to simply stand.
Not to rule, just to be a part of.
Not to take, but to reclaim.
Not to battle, just making you see.
For choice is not a prize to win,
Not a debt, not a sin.
To walk unafraid, to speak, to be
Not less, not more,just equally free.
When no one asks 'why' she dares,
When no one weighs the worth she bears,
Only then, in this raging chaos
Will balance be truly found

21. DEAR YOUNGER SELF

Do not regret the privileges you lacked,
You will have them in abundance later.
Do not regret the sleepless nights of studies,
Everything will make sense in future light.
Do not regret the parties and movies you missed,
You will have plenty of chances,just wait.
Do not regret the constrained love you had,
Love will find you full and free.
Do not regret not being the best every time
You will do good in everything you do.
Do not regret any choices you made,
You led yourself to your life's best.